CONTROVERSIES IN GLOBAL POLITICS & SOCIETIES

REVISITING *PLESSY* AND *BROWN*: WHY "SEPARATE BUT EQUAL" CANNOT BE EQUAL

MOHAMMED SAIF-ALDEN WATTAD
2006/2007 Post-Doctoral Fellow

HALBERT EXCHANGE PROGRAM
at the
MUNK CENTRE
for
INTERNATIONAL STUDIES

MUNK CENTRE FOR INTERNATIONAL STUDIES
UNIVERSITY OF TORONTO

Munk Centre for International Studies
University of Toronto
1 Devonshire Place
Toronto, Ontario, Canada M5S 3K7
Telephone: (416) 946-8900
Facsimile: (416) 946-8915
E-mail: munk.centre@utoronto.ca
Website: www.utoronto.ca/mcis

ISBN 978-0-7727-0833-5
ISSN 1715-3476

Library and Archives Canada Cataloguing in Publication

Wattad, Mohammed Saif-Alden, 1980-
Revisiting *Plessy* and *Brown:* why "separate but equal" cannot be equal /
Mohammed Saif-Alden Wattad

(Controversies in global politics & societies, ISSN 1715-3476 ; VI)
ISBN 978-0-7727-0833-5

1. Equality before the law – United States. 2. Respect for person –
Law and legislation – United States. 3. Discrimination – Law and legislation –
United States. 4. Sociological jurisprudence.
I. Munk Centre for International Studies II. Title. III. Series.
KF4764.W38 2007 342.7308'5 C2007-903010-6

The Munk Centre for International Studies at the University of Toronto seeks to be an internationally recognized leader in interdisciplinary academic research on global issues and to integrate research with teaching and public education. We place special emphasis on the fostering of innovative interdisciplinary knowledge through the exchange of ideas and research among academics as well as the public, private, and voluntary sectors.

HALBERT EXCHANGE PROGRAM
University of Toronto
1 Devonshire Place
Toronto, Ontario, Canada M5S 3K7
E-mail: halbert.munk@utoronto.ca
Website: www.utoronto.ca/halbert

The Halbert Exchange Program, based at the Munk Centre for International Studies in the University of Toronto, is designed to foster and support collaborative research networks between faculty and students from the University of Toronto and The Hebrew University in Jerusalem.

Controversies in Global Politics & Societies

1. *Beyond Nationhood: Citizenship Politics in Germany since Unification.* By Thomas Faist and Triadafilos Triadafilopoulos.
2006 ISBN 0-7727-0824-X

2. *An Institutional Theory of WTO Decision-Making: Why Negotiation in the WTO Resembles Law-Making in the U.S. Congress.* By Gilbert R. Winham.
2006 ISBN 0-7727-0825-8

3. *Official Apologies and the Quest for Historical Justice.* By Michael R. Marrus.
2006 ISBN 0-7727-0826-6

4. *The World Trade Organization: NGOs, New Bargaining Coalitions, and a System under Stress.* By Sylvia Ostry.
2006 ISBN 0-7727-0828-2

5. *The Private Regulation of Global Corporate Conduct.* By David Vogel.
2006 ISBN 0-7727-0831-2

6. *Revisiting* Plessy *and* Brown*: Why "Separate but Equal" Cannot Be Equal.* By Mohammed Saif-Alden Wattad.
2007 ISBN 978-0-7727-0833-5

REVISITING *PLESSY* AND *BROWN*: WHY "SEPARATE BUT EQUAL" CANNOT BE EQUAL

by
MOHAMMED SAIF-ALDEN WATTAD

Plessy and *Brown* represent deep, but also unique, understandings of the intersection between law and society. Equal protection analysis suggests that both are plausible holdings. Equal protection analysis is the wrong path for Americans to take if they want to end discrimination once and for all. For the law to interact successfully with society, the judiciary must understand the meaning of *human dignity*, which focuses on the humiliation that results when people are differentiated on the basis of colour or race. Humiliation results when, under the "separate but equal" doctrine, an individual is treated as a "means" (i.e., as a function of skin colour) rather than as an "end" (i.e., as a function of his or her qualifications).

The author is most grateful to Prof. Patricia Williams, Prof. George P. Fletcher, and Prof. Louis Henkin, all of Columbia Law School; Prof. Lorraine Weinrib of the University of Toronto Faculty of Law; Judge Rosemary Barkett, of the U.S. Court of Appeals for the Eleventh Circuit; and Mr. Saif-Alden Wattad, Adv. and Mr. Ozbej Merc, for reviewing an early draft of this article. My sincere thanks go to Prof. Janice Stein, Dr. Ralph Halbert, Prof. Emanuel Adler, Sylvia Adler and the Munk Centre for their help and support and for providing the environment required to accomplish this work. Without their advice and support none of this would have been possible. Finally, many thanks to Justice Dalia Dorner for her comments and suggestions on the constitutional meaning of the right to dignity. All opinions and errors (and, if applicable, errors of opinion) are my own. The author gratefully acknowledges the comments provided by two anonymous reviewers.

There is no question that human dignity is an indispensable compass in our continuing journey to promote and protect the rights and freedoms of the individual. We may not always know where it will take us, but the fundamental value of human dignity will always remind us where we are coming from.[1]

I. PROLOGUE

"No," he said. "I do not want to be like him. Nor do I want to look like him. All I want is to be free. I do not want to be humiliated. I do not want to be a means. I want to be an end. It is not about his superiority, but about my inferiority. It is not about his privileges, but about the absence of my basic needs. It is not about equality. Nor is it about discrimination. It is all about my dignity."

So far as I can imagine, this would have been Immanuel Kant's argument, had he been asked to argue on behalf of a black racially discriminated person.

II. INTRODUCTION

The American legal system is one of the constitutional legal systems of the Western world.[2] The American Constitution (the Constitution) includes a Bill of Rights, which protects certain fundamental human rights. The United States has a Supreme Court, which is guided by a constitutional oath. That is, the Americans have judicial review.[3] They are not restricted – though this often debated – to interpreting the Constitution solely on its text or by the Framers' intent.[4] Rather, Americans read the Constitution "in light of its full development and its present place in American life throughout the Nation."[5] In light of the Due Process Clause of the Fourteenth Amendment, they have acknowledged the need to recognize certain fundamental unwritten

[1] Dierk Ullrich, "Concurring Visions: Human Dignity in the Canadian Charter of Rights and Freedoms and the Basic Law of the Federal Republic of Germany," 3 (1) *Global Jurist Frontiers* 1 (2003).

[2] Other constitutional systems of the Western world include those of Canada, Germany, South Africa, and Israel.

[3] *Marbury v. Madison*, 1 Cranch, 5 U.S. 137 (1803); *Cooper* v. *Aaron*, 358 U.S. 1 (1958); *Baker v. Carr*, 369 U.S. 186 (1962); Louis Henkin, "Is There a 'Political Question' Doctrine?" 85 *Yale L.J.* 597, 605-606 (1976).

[4] Justice Antonin Scalia supports reading the Constitution as it was originally meant to be read, that is, according to the Framers' intent. He strongly criticizes those who embrace higher principles (viz., natural law) in interpreting the Constitution. See Scalia, "The Rule of the Law as a Law of Rules," 56 *U.Chi.L.Rev.* 1175 (1989).

[5] See *Brown v. Board of Education of Topeka et al.*, 347 U.S. 483, 492-493 (1954).

human rights.[6] They constitutionally protect, inter alia, the freedom of expression,[7] the right to property,[8] the right to life,[9] the right to liberty,[10] the right to equality,[11] and the right to privacy. They have also adopted the doctrine of affirmative action,[12] which encompasses reconciliation vis-à-vis groups they have harmed in the past, thereby sacrificing some of their contemporary glory for the sake of healing their historical national shame.[13]

In addition to all this, they have declared that discriminating against other races – blacks in particular – is unconstitutional. Through the Constitution, they have abolished slavery in all its forms, stating that "[N]either slavery nor involuntary servitude ... shall exist within the United States, or any place subject to their jurisdiction."[14] The height of all this enlightenment was the realization that "separate but equal" is not equal. Such was the famous holding in *Brown*,[15] where the Court rejected the "separate but equal" doctrine upheld in *Plessy*.[16] *Brown* has enriched the Equal Protection Clause of the Fourteenth Amendment, albeit more with constitutional values and anthropomorphism than with constitutional analysis.[17]

To this extent, Americans can be proud of their achievements. They have the right to celebrate their enlightened legal system – a system

[6] This might be called a theory of substantive due process. See, for instance, *Roe v. Wade*, 410 U.S. 113 (1973); *Lawrence v. Texas*, 539 U.S. 558 (2003).
[7] See the First Amendment of the Constitution; *Terminiello v. City of Chicago*, 337 U.S. 1 (1949); *Brandenburg v. Ohio*, 395 U.S. 444 (1969); *National Socialist Party v. Skokie*, 432 U.S. 43 (1977); *Smith v. Collin*, 439 U.S. 916 (1978); *Texas v. Johnson*, 491 U.S. 397 (1989).
[8] See the Fifth and the Fourteenth Amendments of the Constitution.
[9] Ibid.
[10] Ibid. See also Isaiah Berlin, *Four Essays on Liberty* (Oxford: Oxford University Press, 1969); *Allgeyer v. Louisiana*, 165 U.S. 578 (1897).
[11] See the Fifth and the Fourteenth Amendments of the Constitution.
[12] See *Grutter v. Bollinger*, 539 U.S. 982 (2003); *Gratz v. Bollinger*, 539 U.S. 244 (2003).
[13] Later I address the notion of "national shame."
[14] See the Thirteenth Amendment. See also *Brown*, 347 U.S. 483 (1954).
[15] *Brown*, 347 U.S. 483 (1954).
[16] This doctrine was constitutionally upheld by the Supreme Court in *Plessy v. Ferguson*, 163 U.S. 537 (1896). On the history of the "separate but equal" doctrine, see John E. Nowak and Ronald D. Rotunda, *Constitutional Law* 694–706 (6th ed., West Group, 2000); and Gerald Gunther, *Individual Rights in Constitutional Law*, 317–326 (5th ed., Foundation Press, 1992).
[17] In the following sections I show how the analysis in *Brown* of the Equal Protection Clause, unlike that in *Plessy*, goes beyond a simple technical constitutional analysis.

grounded to some degree on "constitutionalism."[18] And celebrate it they do; as one example, recently[19] the Columbia University School of Law held an event to mark the fiftieth anniversary of *Brown*. There, the Honorable Justice Ruth Bader Ginsburg gave a paper on the importance of *Brown* in American constitutional history, ending her address with this acid comment: "If Americans want to be heard by other legal systems, they have mutually to pay attention to foreign legal evolvements."

A comparison of the American legal system with those of other Western countries not only supports the decision in *Brown* but also, and more importantly, suggests an alternative reasoning for it: a reasoning rooted in the right to dignity.[20] Such reasoning "juggles" the right to dignity with the right to equality, to the degree that these two rights share certain constitutional premises.[21] Even so, it is possible as well as useful to examine the right to dignity on its own.

Strangely, the right to dignity does not appear in the American Constitution, even though it is a fundamental principle of constitutions, basic laws, and human rights charters throughout the West.[22] In the twentieth century, that right has become a cornerstone of international and domestic law.[23] An analysis of *Brown* through the lens

[18] By constitutionalism I am not referring merely to constitutional regimes – that is, regimes that rely on a written constitution. I am also referring to regimes that rely as well on natural law (i.e., higher principles). Later I address this issue in depth.

[19] This event took place in 2004.

[20] The following countries (among others) have constitutions that enshrine the right to dignity: Germany, Israel, Canada, and South Africa.

[21] Israel's Basic Law – Human Dignity and Liberty (1992) – explicitly protects the right to dignity as a constitutional right. Though it does not specifically protect the right to equality, it has been held that this latter right is protected under the right to dignity. See S.C.J. 4541/94 *Miller v. Minister of Defense*, P.D. 49(4) 94.

[22] See note 20.

[23] See Article 1(1) of Basic Law for the Federal Republic of Germany (1949; last amended in 1993); Article 4 of the Israeli Basic Law: Human Dignity and Liberty (1992); Article 7(1) of the Constitution of the Republic of South Africa (1996); Articles 5(2), 6(2), and 11(1) of the American Convention on Human Rights (1969); the Preamble of the UN Charter (1945); the Preamble and Article 10(1) of the International Covenant on Civil and Political Rights (1976); and the Preamble of the Universal Declaration of Human Rights (1948). Also, dignity is the general theme of the British Bill of Rights of 1689. Note: While the Canadian Charter of Rights and Freedoms (1982) does not explicitly protect the right to dignity, the Supreme Court of Canada has consistently incorporated it into the Charter through its interpretations, holding that the right to dignity is protected by Article 15(1) of the Charter, which protects the right to equality. See *Miron v. Trudel*, [1995] 2 S.C.R. 418. Akin to this approach, but the other way around, see the Israeli Basic Law: Human Dignity and Liberty (1992), which protects the right to dignity but not the right to equality. On more than one occasion, however, Israel's Supreme Court has held that the right to equality is inherently protected by the right to dignity. See S.C.J. 4541/94 *Miller*, at note 21.

of the right to dignity – whether on its own or conjoined with the right to equality – can provide key insights into what Chief Justice Earl Warren might well have meant when he stated that "to separate them [blacks] from others of similar age and qualifications solely because of their race generates a feeling of inferiority as to their status in the community that may affect their hearts and minds in a way unlikely ever to be undone."[24]

Examining *Brown* – and in particular racial discrimination – through the lens of the right to dignity allows us to approach racial discrimination as a disease rather than merely another constitutional impediment. This analysis does not assert that racial discrimination happens because blacks are treated differently from whites. Rather, it focuses on blacks being humiliated because of their skin colour. Thus it is not a comparative analysis of whites and blacks; the argument, rather, is that blacks are humiliated when they are deemed to be subordinate, inferior, "genetically incorrect." Put simply, this form of humiliation involves treating skin colour as a proxy for rights. Blacks, when humiliated in this way, are a means and not an end, and that is (as Kant understands it) a violation of their human dignity.[25] There is no more humiliating way to treat an individual than as a function of his colour and/or race. This amounts to different or unequal treatment; worse, it is a way to destroy the dignity grounded in the basic tenets of what it is to be human.

I am proposing here a new approach for analyzing *Brown* – one that embodies natural law. Accordingly, I will not be limiting myself to the American Constitution's text. Instead, I will be taking that document to places where it ought to be, rather than simply inquiring into the premises it currently reflects. I will also be approaching racial discrimination as a disease that can be eradicated rather than as a mere constitutional flaw. I will be arguing that dignity, once entrenched as a constitutional right, can immunize society against racism. In comparison, the right to equality is only a temporary cure. The right to dignity and the right to equality have similar effects; the difference is in the length of time they have those

[24] *Brown*, 347 U.S. 483 (1954), at 494.

[25] Later I discuss in depth the Kantian meaning of human dignity.

effects. I will be arguing that the right to dignity holds forever, while the right to equality can only be temporary, because new loopholes will always be found in it that will require ongoing redress. So *Plessy* and *Brown* tell us.

In the first section of this article I offer a brief history of the "separate but equal" argument and discuss the constitutional engines that led to its demise. In the second section I analyze what I call "constitutionalism" and show that every constitutional democratic system includes a trove of human rights that are not necessarily incorporated into constitutional documents. In this way I attempt to locate the right to dignity in the American Constitution as a facet of the right to equality. Finally, I argue that "separate but equal" cannot be equal – that the term at hand is an excuse for treating individuals unequally as a function of their colour and/or race, and in so doing for humiliating them in ways that violate their right to dignity and for that reason are unconstitutional.[26] On the basis of that analysis, I argue that the uncertain promises of the Equal Protection Clause are certain at least as to one – namely, differentiation, which is unconstitutional because it humiliates people of colour, infringes on their right to dignity, humiliates them, and negates their equality. Martin Luther King famously declared: "We must forever conduct our struggle on the high plane of dignity and discipline."[27] This has been elegantly articulated by Derrick Bell:

> The dramatic finale of an extraordinary achievement performed for a nation which had there been a choice would have chosen others, and if given a chance will accept the achievement and neglect the achievers. Here, with simple gesture, they symbolize

[26] The distinction I make between "constitution" and "constitutionalism" and between "constitutional" and "constitutionalist," hinges on the distinction between "is" and "ought," between "the law" and "the Law," and between "written principles" and "higher unwritten principles." "Constitution" and "constitutional" tell us what a written constitution does, what it has, and what it protects. By contrast, "constitutionalism" and "constitutionalist" tell us what a written constitution ought to do, what it ought to have, and what it ought to protect. What are the sources of this "ought"? That is the subject of this article's second section, where I consider the meaning of "constitutionalism" as a theory of legal thinking.

[27] Martin Luther King, Jr., "I Have a Dream," in *The Peaceful Warrior* (Pocket Books, 1968). He delivered this address on the steps of the Lincoln Memorial in Washington, D.C., on August 28, 1963.

> a people whose patience with exploitation will expire with the dignity and certainty with which it has been endured too long.[28]

This approach requires us to think about racism in a way that advances the cure instead of working against it.[29]

III. IS "SEPARATE BUT EQUAL" EQUAL? AN AMERICAN CONSTITUTIONAL STORY

In this section I discuss the sources and the logic of the "separate but equal" doctrine. Once we understand this doctrine and the reasoning behind it, it will be easier for us to understand as well how *Brown* caused its downfall. The "separate but equal" doctrine can be seen as having two poles: *Plessy*[30] at the beginning and *Brown*[31] as the end. So my approach will be to analyze both[32] and explain what underpinned each decision.

The "separate but equal" doctrine goes back to 1890, when Louisiana enacted a statute that declared "that all railway companies shall provide equal but separate accommodations for the whites and colored races."[33] This statute was challenged in the Supreme Court, which found itself having to resolve a clash between the Thirteenth Amendment, which prohibits slavery, and the Fourteenth Amendment, which guards the Equal Protection Clause. The Court found that neither amendment was intended to prohibit "separate but equal" treatment. It then reasoned that the Thirteenth Amendment was intended to abolish slavery as it had been previously known "in this country."[34] Furthermore, the Fourteenth Amendment's main purpose was "to establish the citizenship of the Negro, to give definitions of citizenship of the United States and of the States, and to protect the hostile legislation of the States, the

[28] Derrick Bell, *Race, Racism, and American Law* (5th ed., ASPEN Publishers, 2004). Bell wrote these eloquent words in dedicating his book to all those who throughout America's history have risked its wrath to protest its racism.
[29] Charles R. Lawrence, III, "The ID, the Ego, and Equal Protection: Reckoning with Unconscious Racism," 39 *Stanford Law Review* 317 (1987).
[30] 163 U.S. 537 (1896).
[31] 347 U.S. 483 (1954).
[32] Note: I challenge the "separate but equal" doctrine at the abstract level; at that level, my inquiry and analysis can apply to any assertion of the "separate but equal" doctrine. However, for the purposes of this article, I focus solely on racial discrimination.
[33] *Plessy,* 163 U.S. 537 (1896), at 540.
[34] See *Slaughter-house* cases, 83 U.S. 36 (1873).

privileges, and immunities of citizens of the States."[35] In holding that "separate but equal" can be equal, the Court was grounding its decision – so I argue – on two key statements, which, because of their salience, I will quote at length. I refer to the first of these as the "anti-colourblind" argument:

> A statute which implies merely a legal distinction between the white and colored races – a distinction which is founded in the color of the two races, and which must always exist so long as white men are distinguished from the other race by color – has no tendency to destroy the legal equality of the two races, or reestablish a state of involuntary servitude.[36]

The second statement I refer to as the "equal but without dignity" argument:

> The object of the [Fourteenth] amendment was undoubtedly to enforce the absolute equality of the two races before the law, but in the nature of things it could not have been intended to abolish distinction based upon color, or to enforce social, as distinguished from political equality, or a commingling of the two races upon terms unsatisfactory to either. *Laws permitting, and even requiring, their separation in places where they are liable to be brought into contact, do not necessarily imply the inferiority of either race to the other.*[37]

So theorized the Court on the constitutional meaning of the right to equality. I do not agree with this theory; even so, it is a defensible one under a pure "equal protection" analysis.[38] This decision was not at odds with its time.[39] What *was* at odds was the dissenting opinion by Justice Harlan, who held that "[Our] Constitution is color-blind."[40]

At first glance, one would surmise that the majority of the justices were supporting a policy of racism. That impression would be

[35] Ibid.
[36] *Plessy*, 163 U.S. 537 (1896), at 543.
[37] Ibid., at 544 (emphasis added).
[38] As I show in the next section, this is not the case under a pure "dignity protection" analysis.
[39] For example, see *State v. McCann*, 21 Ohio St. 198 (1871).
[40] *Plessy*, 163 U.S. 537 (1896), at 559.

mistaken. In fact, the Court viewed itself as restricted in its judicial powers – specifically, as having limited judicial review over "social problems." Hence, the *Plessy* ruling, which said in effect that it is not for the Court to promote social change. However,

> [i]f the two races are to meet upon terms of social equality, it must be the result of natural affinities; a mutual appreciation of each other's merits and a voluntary consent of individuals ... this end can neither be accomplished nor promoted by laws which conflict with the general sentiment of the community upon whom they are designed to operate. When the government, therefore, has secured to each of its citizens equal rights before the law and equal opportunities for improvement and progress, it has accomplished the end for which it was organized and performed all of the functions respecting social advantages with which it is endowed.[41]

The fact that this theory would rule for almost six decades, being as strong in 1954 as it was when *Plessy* was rendered, indicates how much jurisprudential scope the Court enjoyed at the time.[42] Not until 1954, in *Brown,*[43] was the Supreme Court able to declare that "separate but equal" is not equal.

In *Brown,* Justice Warren refused to adhere to *Plessy.* The Court challenged the very foundations of *Plessy* – namely, the restrictive reading of the Constitution that limited the Court's power of interpretation to the Framers' intent. Justice Warren provided the Court with a new approach to reading the Constitution:

> [I]n approaching this problem [racial discrimination], we cannot turn the clock back to 1868 when the [Fourteenth] Amendment was adopted, or even to 1896 when *Plessy v. Ferguson* was written. We must consider public education in the light of its full development and its present place in American life throughout the Nation.[44]

41 Ibid., at 551. See also *People v. Gallagher,* 93 N.Y. 438, 448 (1883).
42 I must make it clear that I disagree with the decision and the reasoning in *Plessy.* In the next section I reveal the flaws of this holding and propose an alternative analysis.
43 347 U.S. 483 (1954).
44 Ibid., at 492-493.

Brown signalled a rethinking the "separate but equal" doctrine. But it had been preceded by a series of cases challenging the assertion that "separate but equal" is equal. In *Sweat,* the Court found that a segregated law school for blacks could not provide them with equal educational opportunities. Having held that, the Court considered the case's intangibles, relying on those qualities which cannot be objectively measured but which make for greatness in a law school.[45] In the wake of these decisions, Justice Warren entered calmer waters, where he had only to nudge *Plessy* toward its end. Continuing to address "intangible considerations," he reasoned that the "separate but equal" doctrine had generated among blacks the perception that their social status was inferior, a perception that could affect their hearts and minds. Furthermore, the "separate but equal" doctrine so much as declared that blacks as a group were inferior. From this, it followed that "separate but equal is inherently unequal."[46]

I doubt that this reasoning was derived solely from the right to equality. Fundamentally – and I will soon discuss this point – it was addressing the right to dignity. However, given that the right to dignity does not appear in the Constitution, and given that there is not a single hint that Justice Warren meant to raise the right to dignity, I tend to read his opinion as reflecting another approach to equality rights – one, moreover, that counters the equal protection theory established in *Plessy*. Thus, if I have already supported the *Plessy* decision as a plausible theory of equal protection, here again, in *Brown*, I recognize another such theory. Both *Plessy* and *Brown* can be right. Both are conceivable. And both decisions involved a thorough constitutional analysis of what the right to equality might mean.

Nevertheless, an examination of the analytical method and of the rhetoric of both cases brings to light certain fundamental differences. *Plessy* represented what the Equal Protection Clause was

[45] *Sweat v. Painter et al.*, 339 U.S. 629 (1950). See also *McLaurin v. Oklahoma State Regents for Higher Education*, 339 U.S. 637 (1950).
[46] *Brown*, 347 U.S. 483 (1954), at 495. Justice Warren noted that in the field of public education, the doctrine of "separate but equal" has no place. That is, separate education facilities are inherently unequal. Therefore, segregation is a deprivation of the equal protection of the laws guaranteed by the Fourteenth Amendment.

originally *meant* to be about; by contrast, *Brown* showed what that same clause *ought* to be about. *Plessy* was limited to the text, to history, to the Framers' intent, and to outmoded dogmas,[47] by which I mean what people (however biased) thought to be right. It was limited as well with regard to judicial powers – specifically, it presented a strongly limited notion of judicial review. By contrast, *Brown* provided an extratextual understanding of the Constitution. That is, it interpreted the Constitution beyond the simple meaning of its words;[48] it was an "outward" reading of the Constitution and of its practically intangible meaning. Also, it focused on the attributed inferiority of the victims of segregation policies and thus amounted to a delicate abstract analysis of why "separate but equal" cannot be equal. *Plessy*, by contrast, offered a purely technical reading of the Constitution. Put another way, the victims of segregation played no role in its constitutional analysis, which eschewed the personal. It was the "segregation policy" that the Court examined in *Plessy*; conversely, in *Brown* the victims of segregation were the main actors in the constitutional analysis. The entire story was about *them*: it began with them and ended with them. *Plessy* relied entirely on dry, technical constitutional analysis, whereas *Brown* incorporated an emotional language into the constitutional analysis.

One might view all of this as pointing to a profound difference between *Plessy* and *Brown*. But one could also view any such difference as relating solely to differences over time in the rhetoric of constitutional readings. To this, one might respond that the two cases share the same implicit theme of dignity as the means for locating unconstitutional discrimination. Thus, whereas Justice Brown in *Plessy* held that "laws permitting … their separation … do not necessarily imply the inferiority of their race to the other,"[49]

[47] On the notion of "dogma" and its role in the "law," see George P. Fletcher, "Law, Truth, and Interpretation: A Symposium on Dennis Patterson's Law and Truth: Article: What Law Is Like," 50 *SMU L. Rev.* 1599 (1997).
[48] For arguments for and against the understanding of the "law" in reference to higher principles, see J.E. Ruby, "The Origins of Scientific Law," 47 *Journal of the History of Ideas* 341 (1986); Immanuel Kant, *Critique of Pure Reason* (Norman Kemp-Smith trans., 1964, originally published 1781, Cambridge, Cambridge University Press, 1998); John Austin, *The Province of Jurisprudence Determined* (W. Rumble, ed., 1951, originally published 1832); John Finnis, *Natural Law and Natural Rights* (Clarendon Law Series, Oxford, Oxford University Press, 1980); and Ronald Dworkin, "The Model of Rules," 35 *University of Chicago L. Rev.* 14 (1967).
[49] 163 U.S. 537 (1896), at 544.

Justice Warren in *Brown*, using a similar language, held that "separate but equal" generates feelings of inferiority.[50] Both Justice Brown and Justice Warren agreed, in other words, that "inferiority" is the threshold for ruling on the constitutionality of the "separate but equal" doctrine. Nevertheless, whereas *Plessy* held that "separate but equal" is not always about inferiority, and thus not always unequal, *Brown* held that "separate but equal" is inherently unequal.

To summarize, an equal protection analysis tolerates more than one possible meaning, and various meanings can be normatively plausible even when they contradict one another in their consequences. So, given the implicit analysis of "dignity protection" (which implies "inferiority") in both cases, the question becomes whether an alternative "dignity protection" analysis might offer advantages that an equal protection analysis cannot. I think it can, at least to the extent that it provides a single plausible result rather than a multitude.

IV. CONSTITUTIONALISM, DIGNITY, THE AMERICAN CONSTITUTION, AND THE "SEPARATE BUT EQUAL" DOCTRINE: THE QUEST FOR A THEORY OF LEGAL THINKING

I admit it. The American legal system is a constitutional one. Nonetheless, it is not constitutionalist. In this section I ask, "What is constitutionalism?" I will answer by revisiting *Plessy* and *Brown*. I have already argued that, although an equal protection analysis supports the unconstitutionality of the "separate but equal" doctrine, it can also support its constitutionality, as in *Plessy*. One cannot help feeling that something is inherently wrong with the "separate but equal" doctrine. But what, precisely, *is* wrong with it? Why does it *feel* wrong? Is it shame that we feel, as in *national* shame?[51] If so, it is a shame we feel because we have broken the Constitution's word that all people are created equal, and because those whom we have discriminated against in the past continue to suffer the effects of that

[50] 347 U.S. 483 (1954), at 494.

[51] The notion of national shame is the dominant reason why racial discrimination enjoys strict scrutiny. See *Gratz*, 539 U.S. 244 (2003), at 302. See also *Norwalk Core et al. v. Norwalk Redevelopment Agency et al.*, 395 F.2d 920, 931–932 (CA2 1968), where the court held: "not because [race] is inevitably an impermissible classification, but because it is one which usually, to our national shame, has been drawn for the purpose of maintaining racial inequality."

broken word.[52] Our Constitution declares that no one is superior or inferior with regard to colour, race, gender, and so on – that is, with regard to certain features over which no individual has control. All of this points us toward a discussion about the meaning of human dignity.

In this section, I argue that the "separate but equal" doctrine by definition humiliates individuals by treating them as a function of their colour, race, gender, and so on.[53] Unavoidably, the word "humiliation" draws us into a discussion of the right to dignity – specifically, "human dignity." Clearly, one way to damage a person's dignity is by humiliating that person, by treating him as an object – that is, as a means for achieving other goals – instead of as a subject who bears rights and freedoms – that is, as an end. You humiliate a person by ignoring his qualifications. This argument thus rejects strongly the notion that "separate but equal" is or can ever be equal.

Immanuel Kant and the German theorists on human dignity will be playing a key role in my argument. I would point out here that human dignity plays a paramount role in the jurisprudence of several European countries, including Germany.[54] Also, human dignity has become an important part of the international vocabulary of constitutionalism and human rights.[55]

52 In *United States v. Jefferson County Bd. of Ed.*, 372 F.2d 836, 876 (CA5 1966), the court held: "[T]he Constitution is both colourblind and colour conscious. To avoid conflict with the equal protection clause, a classification that denies a benefit, causes harm, or imposes a burden must not be based on race. In that sense, the Constitution is colourblind. But the Constitution is colour conscious to prevent discrimination being perpetuated and to undo the effects of past discrimination."

53 For the purposes of this article, my argument focuses on race and/or colour.

54 George P. Fletcher, "Human Dignity as a Constitutional Value," 22 *U. W. Ontario L. Rev.* 171 (1984). See also the American Declaration of the Rights and Duties of Man (1992).

55 On the right to dignity and its meaning and importance in constitutional law, see Matthew O. Clifford and Thomas P. Huff, "Some Thoughts on the Meaning and Scope of the Montana Constitution's "Dignity" Clause with Possible Applications," 61 *Mont. L. Rev.* 301 (2000); Laurence H. Tribe, "Essay: *Lawrence v. Texas:* The "Fundamental Right" That Dare Not Speak Its Name," 117 *Harv. L. Rev.* 1893 (2004); Edward J. Eberle, "Human Dignity, Privacy, and Personality in German and American Constitutional Law," 1997 *Utah L. Rev.* 963 (1997); Vicki C. Jackson, "Constitutional Dialogue and Human Dignity: States and Transnational Constitutional Discourse," 65 *Mont. L. Rev.* 15 (2004); Heidi Joy Schmid, "Decriminalizing of Somebody Under South Africa's 1996 Constitution: Implications for South Africa and U.S. Law," 8 *Cardozo J. Int'l & Comp. L.* 163 (2000); and Kevin Brown, "Do African Americans Need Immersion Schools?: The Paradoxes Created by Legal Conceptualization of Race and Public Education," 78 *Iowa L. Rev.* 813 (1993).

However, what might be best for Germany, and for many other Western legal systems, as well as for international constitutional entities, might not be best for American constitutional law. Unlike other constitutions, the American Constitution provides no protection for human dignity, either by an explicit reference or through the resulting interpretations.[56] Nowhere does it refer specifically to human dignity.[57] Even so, "dignity" is not an exotic beast in American jurisprudence. For example, the Constitution itself contains some cognate concepts, including these:

- The ban on cruel and unusual punishment.[58] This implicitly calls for mercy toward criminals and thus views them as ends – that is, as human beings – rather than as means of criminal laws and procedures.
- The protection of the Due Process Clause.[59] The focus here is on legal procedures: that is, on their goals and how they are to be achieved.[60]

The term "human dignity" made its first appearance in the U.S. Reports in 1946, in Justice Murphy's dissent in *In re Yamashita.*[61] Martin Luther King was the first to propose that human dignity has its basis in natural law:

[56] See note 23.
[57] Note: The Montana Supreme Court interpreted its state constitution as protecting the right to dignity within Article II, Section 10, of the Montana Constitution of 1972, which guarantees the right to privacy. The court held that in addition to its Section 10 guarantee of privacy, Article II includes a guarantee of individual dignity. This guarantee avows: "The dignity of the human being is inviolable." See *Stratemeyer v. MACO Workers' Comp. Trust,* 259 Mont. 147, 155, 855 P.2d, 511–512 (1993), where Justice Trieweiler wrote in his dissenting opinion that the dignity of the human being is inviolable, and thus no person shall be denied equal protection of the laws. Yet the purpose served by that language in any society based on equality is absolutely vital. It recognizes that majoritarian rule can at times be harsh, intolerant, and unfair. It recognizes that at times a basic framework of principles is necessary to prevent those with political influence from oppressing those without it. See also Clifford and Huff, at note 55.
[58] See the Eighth Amendment of the American Constitution.
[59] See the Fourteenth Amendment of the American Constitution.
[60] For other concepts that have been developed by the U.S. Supreme Court, see Jackson, at note 55.
[61] *In re Yamashita,* 327 U.S. 1, 29 (1946): "If we are ever to develop an orderly international community based upon a recognition of human dignity it is of utmost importance that the necessary punishment of those guilty of atrocities be as free as possible from the ugly stigma of revenge and vindictiveness."

Unjust law is no law at all ... A just law is a man-made code that squares with the moral law or the law of God. An unjust law is a code that is out of harmony with the moral law ... Any unjust law is a human law that is not rooted in eternal law and natural law, any law that uplifts human personality is just. *Any law that degrades human personality is unjust.*[62]

Human dignity, then, is a core component of constitutional jurisprudence in a constitutional system. It is the most basic and foundational of rights. Yet human dignity in modern society is an elusive goal,[63] mainly because it is so difficult to define. Human dignity is a broad concept, and thus it is difficult to determine precisely what it means. We can, though, say some things about it. In terms of individuals, we can think of dignity as the ability to pursue one's rights, claims, and interests in daily life so that one can fully realize one's talents, ambitions, and abilities.[64] A common term for this is self-realization. What matters here is that each person should be free to develop his own being to the fullest. One could suggest that "human dignity" can mean many things.[65] Yet at a minimum, it calls on the social order to recognize the equality of humankind,[66] which means at the very least that all people are entitled to "equal worth"[67] – and is this not the meaning of human dignity? It is the bedrock understanding that all people are created equal and are entitled to be treated as such. People might rightfully be treated unequally because of their qualifications, but not as human beings. As human beings, they are entitled to equal worth, whatever their colour, race, gender, and so on.

[62] Martin Luther King, "Letter from Birmingham Jail," 26(4) *U.C. Davis L. Rev.* 835, 840 (1993) (emphasis added).
[63] See Eberle, at note 55.
[64] See Immanuel Kant, *Metaphysics of Morals* 39 (L.W. Beck trans., 2d ed., 1959). Cf. John Rawls, *Political Liberalism* (Columbia University Press, 1993); Ronald Dworkin, *Taking Rights Seriously* (Harvard University Press, 1977); idem, *Law's Empire* (Belknap Press of Harvard University Press, 1986); Robert Nozick, *Anarchy, State, and Utopia* (Basil Blackwell, 1974); and Anthony Sampson, *The Changing Anatomy of Britain* (Random House, 1982).
[65] Other meanings might include (1) respect for physical identity and integrity and (2) respect for intellectual and spiritual identity and integrity.
[66] See Eberle, at note 55, at 975.
[67] See note 65.

Dignity is a unique feature of humankind. It is what distinguishes human beings from other animals. Those who lose this dignity are no longer human, as they have lost that supreme value that differentiates humans from animals. Dignity cannot survive once human beings have been humiliated – that is, once they have been treated as means rather than ends. Humiliation is the most crippling possible way to deprive human beings of what they are. In a world in which human dignity had no inherent special meaning, I doubt whether any other human values or rights could exist, including the right to liberty and the right to life itself. Human beings as unique entities are destroyed when a state grants itself the power to distinguish between human beings based on attributes such as skin colour. This is a barbarous way of treating human beings, and in any constitutionalist society, it would result in there being no life. However, before we accuse the United States of treating its black citizens barbarically, it is vital that we locate human dignity in the American Constitution, which does not explicitly protect human dignity.

The American Constitution does not exist in a vacuum. It is part of a broader theory of constitutionalism, a theory that purports to address how a constitution ought to be read, understood, and interpreted.[68] This theory rejects any attempt to turn the clock back to early times or to merely reflect back what the text or the drafters meant to say. In other words, the constitution is a living document[69] that does not rely on the past. It does not blindly follow those who wrote it; rather, it draws necessary conclusions from what is not working in the present day and in so doing draws lessons for the future. The distinction I make between "constitution" and "constitutionalism" is part of my effort to distinguish between the *is* and the *ought*. A constitution is a written document that tells us what it does, what it has, and what it protects. By contrast, constitutionalism tells us what a written constitutional document ought to do, what it ought to have, and what it ought to protect. What, then, are the sources of this *ought*? This is precisely the question that is addressed by the constitutionalism theory as a theory of legal thinking.

[68] See note 48.

[69] See note 4. See also *Rummel v. Estelle*, 445 U.S. 263 (1980); *National League of Cities v. Usery*, 426 U.S. 833 (1976); William H. Rehnquist, "The Notion of a Living Constitution," 54 *Tex. L. Rev.* 693 (1976); Charles A. Reich, "Mr. Justice Black and the Living Constitution," 76 *Harv. L. Rev.* 673, (1963); and James Gray Pope, "Labor-Community Coalitions and Boycotts: The Old Labor Law, the New Unionism, and the Living Constitution," *69 Tex. L. Rev. 889* (1991).

Human rights occupies a vast area of present-day legal discourse, especially in constitutional law. When he referred to the concepts of human rights, just law, moral values, and natural law, as well as to the concept that "all people were created equal,"[70] Martin Luther King was relying on a sweeping philosophical concept: that human rights have a natural origin and must be protected.[71] This concept slices to the core of legal thinking.[72]

Most documents refer to an abstract power as the source of all human rights, and in this way to the requirement to protect those rights. This assertion of an abstract power is what grounds theories about ideal notions of human rights. In the modern world – that is, the materialist world – this ideal has been reshaped by philosophers, who would impose certain duties on the state, as an entity of organizing power, to protect human rights. However, in a political collective – that is, a state – rights cannot be absolute. There are always other legitimate social and political interests, as well as other conflicting rights. In the clash between these rights and interests, the state must find a balance. So it is right that there be no absolute rights. But it is also true that the state's power, being derived from the "will of the people," can only impose limits on human rights for the sake of achieving other legitimate goals. That is, its impositions

70 See Martin Luther King, at note 27.

71 See, for example, the English Bill of Rights (1689); the Declaration of Independence of the United States of America (1776); the United States Constitution (1787); The Basic Law for the Federal Republic of Germany (promulgated by the Parliamentary Council on 23 May 1949, last amended 1990); the French Declaration of the Rights of Man and of the Citizen (1789); the French Constitution (1958); the Canadian Charter of Rights and Freedoms (1982); the Israeli Basic Law: Human Dignity and Liberty (1992); and the Constitution of the Republic of South Africa (1996).

72 See Patrick Hayden, *The Philosophy of Human Rights* (Paragon House, 2001). In particular see his accounts of Cicero, at 34; St. Thomas Aquinas, at 43; Thomas Hobbes, at 57; John Locke, at 71; Jean-Jacques Rousseau, at 80; Thomas Paine, at 95; H.L.A. Hart, at 151; Joel Feinberg, at 174; and Abdullahi Ahmed An-Na'im, at 315. See also John Rawls, *A Theory of Justice* (rev. ed., Belknap Press of Harvard University Press, 1999); the Universal Declaration of Human Rights (1948); the Declaration on the Rights on Individuals, Groups, and Organs of Society to Promote and Protect Universally Recognized Human Rights and Fundamental Freedoms (1998); the European Convention for Protection of Human Rights and Fundamental Freedoms (1950); the European Union Charter of Fundamental Rights (2000); the American Declaration of the Rights and Duties of Man (1948); the American Convention on Human Rights (1969); the African Charter on Human and People's Rights (1981); the Cairo Declaration on Human Rights in Islam (1990); and the Arab Charter on Human Rights (1994). See also Ian Brownlie and Guy Goodwin-Gill, *Basic Documents on Human Rights* (4th ed., Oxford University Press, 2002). See also Genesis 5. The Magna Carta (1215) also refers to God.

cannot extend to erasing those rights to the point that they never existed. Thus, a state may limit the right to free expression, but it cannot abolish that right. Furthermore, there may be certain rights that by their nature cannot be limited, for to limit them would be to nullify them. Such rights either exist or do not.[73] They include the right to life[74] and, I believe, the right to dignity. Let me focus on the right to dignity.

The American Constitution provides that it[75] shall be the supreme law of the land.[76] This is not right. It is not true. And it can be neither right nor true. The legal-philosophical distinction between "law" and "Law" is based not on a declaratory statement of the legislature, but rather on an essential mechanism for recognizing rights and freedoms. It is the distinction between the rule of unwritten principles[77] and the rule of statutory principles.[78] Therefore, for the American Constitution to become the supreme law of the

[73] I am aware that this argument has consistently been rejected by the U.S. Supreme Court and by all other legal systems. See *Jacobson v. Massachusetts,* 197 U.S. 11 (1905); and *Buck v. Bell,* 274 U.S. 200 (1927). However, my argument relies on a theory of legal thought, which I refer to as "constitutionalism," which I developed earlier. In this article I address several aspects of this theory, but it is for another analysis to spread out the whole theory. For the purposes of this article, it is sufficient to raise the argument.

[74] This argument emerges from another discussion on the constitutionality of capital punishment. However, that is not the subject of this article, and thus I leave it for another inquiry.

[75] And in addition, the laws of the United States and all treaties made under the authority of the United States.

[76] Article VI of the Constitution.

[77] David Jenkins, "From Unwritten to Written: Transformation in the British Common Law Constitution," 36 *Vand. J. Transnat'l L.* 863 (2003); Nathan N. Frost, Rachel Beth Klein-Levine, and Thomas B. McAffee, "Courts over Constitutions Revisited: Unwritten Constitutionalism in the State," 2004 *Utah L. Rev.* 333 (2004); Luc B. Tremblay, "A Round Table on American Constitutional Law: *Marbury v. Madison:* History, Legitimacy, Influence: *Marbury v. Madison* and Canadian Constitutionalism: Rhetoric and Practice," 37 *R.J.T.* 375 (2003). See also George P. Fletcher, *Basic Concepts of Legal Thought,* 11–27 (Oxford University Press, 1996). Professor George Fletcher argues, and I agree, that the rule of law flourishes when power is expressed in orderly bureaucratic behaviour. Thus the law takes the place of the authority expressed by parents, teachers, and philosophers. The philosophy of the human right is the basis for the supremacy of the "rule of law" as the "Good and Just Law." Searching for the sources of the idea of "Law," he presents three: (1) the analogy between scientific laws and human laws, which lends certain formal criteria to the laws that govern social life; (2) the notion of higher law that injects an element of morality to living under law; and (3) the ancient idea that law is the path on which the community travels as an organic unit. In Fletcher's mind, in any given society all three sources converge in generating a complex legal culture.

[78] See Scalia, at note 4; Joseph Raz, "The Rule of Law and Its Virtue," in Raz, *The Authority of Law: Essays on Law and Morality,* 210 (Oxford University Press, 1979).

land, it is not enough that it be located, normatively, at the top of a hierarchy of norms; rather, it must be subject to constitutionalism theory, which encompasses what Justice Warren called "intangible considerations."[79] These are higher principles that demand the incorporation of certain values and fundamental rights – at the very least individual human rights – into any constitutional regime. Otherwise, that regime would not be constitutionalist.

The point is this: The right to dignity is not in the American Constitution, but this does *not* mean it should *not* be there. Constitutionalism would require that it be there. Given the importance of human dignity, the right to dignity ought to be in the American Constitution. It could be included simply by referring to "intangible considerations"[80] or "higher principles," or by establishing an explicit right to dignity through mechanisms of interpretation. I would prefer the latter option, which would be direct, plain, and sharply challenging.

As I read the American Constitution, I recognize three premises through which the right to dignity could be naturally incorporated. These are the Ninth Amendment, the Due Process Clause, and the Equal Protection Clause (the latter two under the Fourteenth Amendment).

The Ninth Amendment provides that "the enumeration in the Constitution, of certain rights, shall not be construed to deny or disparage others retained by the people." Does that include the right to dignity? I contend that, although the Ninth Amendment has received almost no serious attention by the Supreme Court, it may establish the core of my constitutionalist theory under the American Constitution, for it recognizes non-listed rights that are retained by the people.[81]

To date, the Ninth Amendment has been successfully invoked only in *Griswold*,[82] where the Supreme Court held that a state anti-birth control statute was an unconstitutional invasion of the

[79] *Brown*, 347 U.S. 483 (1954), at 494.
[80] Ibid.
[81] This idea gives even normative power to the Preamble, which refers to the People as the legitimacy of the United States Constitution.
[82] See *Griswold et al. v. Connecticut*, 381 U.S. 479 (1965).

right to marital privacy. This right, though not specified under the Bill of Rights, was nevertheless among those rights "retained by the people," to which the Ninth Amendment alludes. Following this holding, on its face, if the right to marital privacy is recognized as a retained right by the people, all the more so the right to dignity. This is a conceivable reading of the Ninth Amendment as a general recognition of inherent or natural rights.[83]

But this is only one pillar for establishing the right to dignity within the premises of the American Constitution. The second pillar is the Due Process Clause of the Fourteenth Amendment, which has been interpreted as granting constitutional protection to "fundamental rights" even when those rights are not expressly protected by the Constitution.[84] It is just as obvious, then, that the right to dignity is the most fundamental of rights and that it ought to be protected by the substantive meaning of the Due Process Clause. The right to privacy is already granted this privilege, and that right cannot be more fundamental than the right to dignity, especially since the former is at least partly derived from the latter.

The third and final pillar – and I would say the most important – is the Equal Protection Clause. This clause is the most compatible with the right to dignity and provides certain premises from which that right can arise. Human dignity features prominently in the equality guarantee in the American Constitution. (Bear in mind here that this article is about the right to dignity *and* the right to equality, which have similar origins.[85]) As mentioned earlier, the core meaning of dignity is that the social order must reflect the equal worth of all people.[86] Dignity expresses at least the basic meaning of equality.[87]

We know at this point what dignity means. At least, we know when it is absent, and that it is absent when we humiliate a person by

[83] Norman Redlich, "Are There 'Certain Rights … Retained by the People'?" 37 *New York University Law Review* 787 (1962).
[84] On the scope of the Due Process Clause as a guarantee for the constitutional protection of unwritten fundamental human rights, see *Roe*, 410 U.S. 113.
[85] See Ullrich, at note 1.
[86] Other meanings might be (1) respect for physical identity and integrity, or (2) respect for intellectual and spiritual identity and integrity.
[87] Similarly, see the second clause of Article II, Section 4, of the Montana Constitution, which provides a similar notion of the Equal Protection Clause of the Fourteenth Amendment.

treating him as a means and not an end. Yet we still do not know what equality means. This compels us to ask: How are humiliation and dignity related to notions of equal protection?

The equality principle is key to constitutional jurisprudence and democratic regimes. According to the Constitution's reading of "unlawful discrimination," treating people differently is not the same as treating them unequally. Unlawful discrimination encompasses treating people differently who are equally qualified, which is obviously unfair. So not every differentiation made between two individuals is unlawful discrimination – or more accurately, "unlawful differentiation." Sometimes differentiation is justified owing to differences that exist between two persons. The equality principle is based on "relevantism," by which I mean it is acceptable to differentiate between two individuals on the basis of relevant considerations, whereas it is not acceptable to do so on the grounds of non-relevant considerations. But there are times when differentiation stigmatizes individuals, especially when the differentiation is based on something collective, such as race, gender, colour, or religion. This raises the issue of whether an argument of "separate but equal" points to the sort of differentiation that causes this kind of stigma. To answer this question, one must ask first: What do we mean by "separate but equal"?

The "separate but equal" policy says: "It is not that I don't want to live in this neighbourhood, it is that I don't want to live with you." The focus in that statement is not on the neighbourhood, nor is it about the superiority of the one who is speaking. Rather, it is about the inferiority of one party, one group, or some individuals. It is about subordination, especially when those who are being spoken to are a collective or an isolated minority. And it is about disparaging the human spirit. When one talks about a collective, one leaves no place for the individual, no matter what that person's qualifications. That person is being prejudged solely on the basis of his affiliation with a certain group. This sort of treatment may raise the legal argument in favour of pure equal protection, mainly because this is what we can see – that is, differentiation based on the relevance of one or another group. What we *cannot* see, but what the victim *feels*, is the insult, or the affront that sharpens the differences between the two groups. That is to say, the insult is aimed not at the person but at the group. The individual's feelings are ignored; he is merely an instrument for talking about and treating the collective. The individual is nothing but a means. He is – and in this context one could just as easily say "it is" – not an end. He is not a purpose in himself. This is the "classic" method of humiliation. I can think of no better example of the "separate but equal" policy at work than humiliating a person while pretending not to.

The "separate but equal" doctrine, when played out like this, sends a message that the recipient is inferior or even inherently subordinate, and this cannot but stigmatize that individual as inferior. A vicious circle then arises that perpetuates the differentiation. The stigma of inferiority, especially when grounded in biological differences, leads to differentiation, which then corroborates and supports the degrading stereotype. The basic purpose, then, of racial differentiation is to humiliate the victim, and that is a severe infringement on the constitutional right to dignity, which is, in this case, a proxy for equal protection. There is no way to formulate a constitutional analysis by which "separate but equal" would not result in humiliation and thereby generate a violation of the right to dignity. It follows that "separate but equal" is not equal, and cannot be equal, and ought not be equal.

V. CONCLUSION: DIGNITY AS A TREATMENT FOR THE DISEASE OF RACIAL DISCRIMINATION

> *Man kann von* einem *Ding nicht aussagen, es sei 1 m lang, noch, es sei nicht 1 m lang, und das ist das Urmeter in Paris.*
> *(There is one thing of which one can say neither that it is one metre long, nor that it is not one metre long, and that is the standard metre in Paris.)*[88]

Many social criteria are viewed as absolute when in fact they are arbitrary. Yet not all arbitrary criteria are as arbitrary as the "standard metre in Paris." There are times when it is possible – and when possible, only right – to determine just criteria.

In this article I have discussed the criteria for translating supposed differences between whites and blacks into legal norms. These

[88] Ludwig Wittgenstein, *Philosophy: The German Text, with a Revised English Translation* Pt. I, §50 (3rd ed., trans. G.E.M. Anscombe, Blackwell, 2001).

criteria can and should be just. But they can be so only if we confront the supposed differences in order to understand the disgrace that is built into them.

The American people have a complicated history in racial matters. Step by step they have built a constitutional regime in which they can take pride – for example, the adoption of the Bill of Rights. American history has been one long story of the good vanquishing the bad. The American people aspired to become "a more perfect union" and have often succeeded.[89] Martin Luther King's "I Have a Dream" speech was a defining moment in this journey.[90] Yet the Reverend King was not dreaming about *equality* in that address; rather, he was dreaming about human dignity as the direct opposite of humiliation. By expressing this dream, he awakened the American people to a new era, one in which human beings would be treated as ends rather than as means. Case by case, the courts have opened the path toward his dream. The Bill of Rights, adopted by the Constitution in 1791, had been only the first step. The next important ones were the Due Process Clause and the Equal Protection Clause,[91] which advanced the recognition of fundamental human rights, which had not till then been expressly protected by the Constitution.

Yet what would have been a key development in constitutional law did not follow these advances. Maintaining their loyalty to certain outmoded practices, Americans have failed to protect human rights when it would have been easy for them to do so. And the reason they have not is that the American Constitution does not protect the right to dignity.

The United States is not the only constitutional legal system in the Western world, but it is among the leading ones. Yet the United States is one of the only *non*-constitutionalist systems in the West, in the sense that it maintains its loyalty to the Framer's intent instead of embracing higher unwritten principles of natural law. I am not suggesting that the American Constitution is blind to human rights;

[89] See Preamble of the American Constitution.
[90] See note 27.
[91] See Section 1 of the Fourteenth Amendment of the American Constitution.

I *am* saying that it is not yet a *constitutionalist* constitution. All constitutions, including the American Constitution, and even those which are crafted solely to be ignored, include a language of human rights. Moreover, all constitutions are unique when we examine them closely enough. This uniqueness is what I refer to as "constitutionalism." Many states have embraced this uniqueness, and others are making efforts to do so; only the United States has consistently failed in this.

I realize what I am contending here, and I admit that hints of implicit recognition of constitutionalism emerge from time to time in American jurisprudence.[92] However, the United States has never adopted the mechanisms that would enable it to rise to constitutionalist vehicles such as the Canadian, the German, the Israeli constitutions, and even the constitution of the reborn Republic of South Africa. Remarkably, the American is the oldest of all constitutionalist systems yet it is not the most advanced of them.

When I looked into the history of American constitutional law, I was taken aback by its "laziness." True, American constitutional law is not static. And even more true, there is nothing wrong with a system being cautious or with it proceeding by increments. Yet even in that light, American constitutional law is very far from dynamic. When we view the Framers' intent in terms of the past and constitutionalism in terms of the future, the basic feature of American constitutional evolution is its propensity to reach toward the future *through* the past. If constitutions and the protection of human rights are about enlightenment, and I believe they are, this should not be how constitutions evolve. History is a place we can never visit and thus should not try to visit. For every moment we spend thinking[93] about history, we plunder a moment from our future. For a living constitution, history is the backwards direction. For a constitution to live, it must be culturally and contextually relevant. A constitution must be timeless; it must amount to a new beginning; it must turn its back on the dark for the sake of the light.

[92] Such as the development of "substantive due process," through which unwritten fundamental rights can be incorporated.

[93] This is unlike "rethinking," which I indeed recommend. By "rethinking" we recognize our historical national shame and become able to realize what our future goals must be. "Historical rethinking" is a proxy for enlightened and lightened future.

American constitutional law has always moved at a glacier's pace. For example, legal slavery ended in the rest of the world long before it ended in the United States. And even then, the Americans replaced it with their newly coined "separate but equal" doctrine, which lived for almost six decades before the Supreme Court in *Brown* held that "separate but equal" is inherently unequal. That was a revolutionary and enriching moment for American constitutional law. One would have expected this development to open a new era for the judiciary *and* for society, but this was an elusive hope, for several reasons. First, there was a wide gap between what the Court judged to be right and what the American people deemed *ought* to be right. Second, and more importantly, this elusive revolution was hardly smooth – in fact, it was strongly resisted. That is not to say there was no revolution at all, and I doubt whether the American legal system would have reached its present state without this revolution. My point is that this revolution was not strong enough. It was not brave. It did not finish what it started. Implicitly, it treated racial discrimination as a disease; but it lacked the courage to say so expressly. This was a revolution launched by a technical analysis of the Constitution, though ultimately it was driven by intangibles. For all of these reasons, it did not eradicate the disease, but only relieved its symptoms for a time. As a consequence, the United States will continue to face this disease again and again in the future.

In contrast, an abstract analysis, one that looks deep into the causes of a disease with the goal of rooting it out, would have a much stronger impact. But that, you might argue, would require a constitutionalist mechanism – that is, something capable of showing us clearly what the disease is and where it is located. This mechanism would be capable of addressing the appearance of discrimination; but more than this, it would be able to penetrate the problem's body and touch its heart and mind. Simply put, this mechanism can be only the right to dignity, which by its nature is able to reflect what people feel. The problem is that the concept of dignity is not explicitly written in the American Constitution. It is not even thought to be there. No binding authority has recognized it, at least expressly, or even suggested that it ought to be there. Why is this so?

The American Constitution has a genetic defect – I apologize for this metaphor, but I cannot find a more suitable one. A constitution that offers no meaning of dignity can have no idea what constitutionalism is all about. Moreover, a constitution that ties its future to its history cannot help but clash with itself. And to argue that "if the two races are to meet upon terms of social equality ... this end can neither be accomplished nor promoted by laws,"[94] is to betray a flawed understanding of what constitutional democracy (as distinguished from parliamentary democracy) ought to do. In a legal system governed by constitutional democracy, the legislature does not act merely to reflect the majority opinion.[95] Rather, it drives two mechanisms of checks and balances – those between the three governmental branches, and those between the majority interests and the minority interests. Without this mechanism the minority's interests would be less protected (if at all) than the interests of the majority. The majority is able to express its power through the ballot box, whereas minorities are "muted"; this is why it is so necessary for the judiciary, in a constitutional democracy, to speak on behalf of them, insofar as neither the legislature nor the government is likely to do so.

Americans do not lack a concept of constitutional law; they do, though, lack an accurate understanding of it, and as a result their Constitution is flawed. Flawed, but not blind. Constitutional law is a universal concept marked by high principles and an internationalist world view. Furthermore, it does not live in a vacuum. Nor is it limited to certain eras, or to certain nations, or to certain words and phrases. For example, "due process" is not just two empty words; it has a powerful and universal resonance once one thoroughly *understands* those words. Unfortunately, none of this is reflected in the U.S. Supreme Court's approach to the right to dignity or – it follows – in its treatment for the "separate but equal" disease. Here, let me take some advice from a child. If you give a child a loaf of bread, he will start eating it from the inside – that is, he will begin with the body of the loaf rather than the crust. Like children, in order to eradicate racial discrimination, we need to start by treating the problem from the inside, beginning with the right to dignity, rather than from the outside, with the right to equality. But this does not mean that the two are not connected.

[94] *Plessy*, 163 U.S. 537 (1896), at 551.
[95] Parliamentary democracy is ruled by majority decisions.

Finally, we cannot treat a disease successfully unless we recognize it exists. Only having done that can we cure it. Awareness is crucial to successful treatment. Similarly, we must make ourselves aware of why "separate but equal" cannot be equal.[96] This is the correct path for a democracy to take that purports to protect human rights. If it does not, it cannot be honest with itself or the world.

> So Jacob went near to Isaac his father, who felt him and said, "The voice is Jacob's voice, but the hands are the hands of Esau." And he did not recognize him, because his hands were hairy like his brother Esau's hands; so he blessed him. He said, "Are you really my son Esau?" He answered, "I am." Then he said, "Bring it to me, that I may eat of my son's game and bless him..."[97]

[96] See Lawrence, at note 29.
[97] Genesis 27:21–25.